RECIPE JOURNAL

Blank Cookbook To Write In

This Book Belongs To

_____

Contents

No	Recipe Name	Page	Star Rating

Contents

No	Recipe Name	Page	Star Rating

Contents

No	Recipe Name	Page	Star Rating

Contents

No	Recipe Name	Page	Star Rating

Contents

No	Recipe Name	Page	Star Rating

Contents

No	Recipe Name	Page	Star Rating

Contents

No	Recipe Name	Page	Star Rating

Recipe Name			
Serves	Prep Time	Cooking Time	Oven Temp

Ingredients

Directions

Notes

Recipe Name			
Serves	Prep Time	Cooking Time	Oven Temp

Ingredients

Directions

Notes

Recipe Name			
Serves	Prep Time	Cooking Time	Oven Temp

Ingredients

Directions

Notes

Recipe Name			
Serves	Prep Time	Cooking Time	Oven Temp

Ingredients

Directions

Notes

Recipe Name			
Serves	Prep Time	Cooking Time	Oven Temp

Ingredients

Directions

Notes

Recipe Name			
Serves	Prep Time	Cooking Time	Oven Temp

Ingredients

Directions

Notes

Recipe Name			
Serves	Prep Time	Cooking Time	Oven Temp

Ingredients

Directions

Notes

Recipe Name			
Serves	Prep Time	Cooking Time	Oven Temp

Ingredients

Directions

Notes

Recipe Name			
Serves	Prep Time	Cooking Time	Oven Temp

Ingredients

Directions

Notes

Recipe Name			
Serves	Prep Time	Cooking Time	Oven Temp

Ingredients

Directions

Notes

Recipe Name			
Serves	Prep Time	Cooking Time	Oven Temp

Ingredients

Directions

Notes

Recipe Name			
Serves	Prep Time	Cooking Time	Oven Temp

Ingredients

Directions

Notes

Recipe Name			
Serves	Prep Time	Cooking Time	Oven Temp

Ingredients

Directions

Notes

Recipe Name			
Serves	Prep Time	Cooking Time	Oven Temp

Ingredients

Directions

Notes

Recipe Name			
Serves	Prep Time	Cooking Time	Oven Temp

Ingredients

Directions

Notes

Recipe Name			
Serves	Prep Time	Cooking Time	Oven Temp

Ingredients

Directions

Notes

Recipe Name			
Serves	Prep Time	Cooking Time	Oven Temp

Ingredients

Directions

Notes

Recipe Name			
Serves	Prep Time	Cooking Time	Oven Temp

Ingredients

Directions

Notes

Recipe Name			
Serves	Prep Time	Cooking Time	Oven Temp

Ingredients

Directions

Notes

Recipe Name			
Serves	Prep Time	Cooking Time	Oven Temp

Ingredients

Directions

Notes

Recipe Name			
Serves	Prep Time	Cooking Time	Oven Temp

Ingredients

Directions

Notes

Recipe Name			
Serves	Prep Time	Cooking Time	Oven Temp

Ingredients

Directions

Notes

Recipe Name			
Serves	Prep Time	Cooking Time	Oven Temp

Ingredients

Directions

Notes

Recipe Name			
Serves	Prep Time	Cooking Time	Oven Temp

Ingredients

Directions

Notes

Recipe Name			
Serves	Prep Time	Cooking Time	Oven Temp

Ingredients

Directions

Notes

Recipe Name			
Serves	Prep Time	Cooking Time	Oven Temp

Ingredients

Directions

Notes

Recipe Name			
Serves	Prep Time	Cooking Time	Oven Temp

Ingredients

Directions

Notes

Recipe Name			
Serves	Prep Time	Cooking Time	Oven Temp

Ingredients

Directions

Notes

Recipe Name			
Serves	Prep Time	Cooking Time	Oven Temp

Ingredients

Directions

Notes

Recipe Name			
Serves	Prep Time	Cooking Time	Oven Temp

Ingredients

Directions

Notes

Recipe Name			
Serves	Prep Time	Cooking Time	Oven Temp

Ingredients

Directions

Notes

Recipe Name			
Serves	Prep Time	Cooking Time	Oven Temp

Ingredients

Directions

Notes

Recipe Name			
Serves	Prep Time	Cooking Time	Oven Temp

Ingredients

Directions

Notes

Recipe Name			
Serves	Prep Time	Cooking Time	Oven Temp

Ingredients

Directions

Notes

Recipe Name			
Serves	Prep Time	Cooking Time	Oven Temp

Ingredients

Directions

Notes

Recipe Name			
Serves	Prep Time	Cooking Time	Oven Temp

Ingredients

Directions

Notes

Recipe Name			
Serves	Prep Time	Cooking Time	Oven Temp

Ingredients

Directions

Notes

Recipe Name			
Serves	Prep Time	Cooking Time	Oven Temp

Ingredients

Directions

Notes

Recipe Name			
Serves	Prep Time	Cooking Time	Oven Temp

Ingredients

Directions

Notes

Recipe Name			
Serves	Prep Time	Cooking Time	Oven Temp

Ingredients

Directions

Notes

Recipe Name			
Serves	Prep Time	Cooking Time	Oven Temp

Ingredients

Directions

Notes

Recipe Name			
Serves	Prep Time	Cooking Time	Oven Temp

Ingredients

Directions

Notes

Recipe Name			
Serves	Prep Time	Cooking Time	Oven Temp

Ingredients

Directions

Notes

Recipe Name			
Serves	Prep Time	Cooking Time	Oven Temp

Ingredients

Directions

Notes

Recipe Name			
Serves	Prep Time	Cooking Time	Oven Temp

Ingredients

Directions

Notes

Recipe Name			
Serves	Prep Time	Cooking Time	Oven Temp

Ingredients

Directions

Notes

Recipe Name			
Serves	Prep Time	Cooking Time	Oven Temp

Ingredients

Directions

Notes

Recipe Name			
Serves	Prep Time	Cooking Time	Oven Temp

Ingredients

Directions

Notes

Recipe Name			
Serves	Prep Time	Cooking Time	Oven Temp

Ingredients

Directions

Notes

Recipe Name			
Serves	Prep Time	Cooking Time	Oven Temp

Ingredients

Directions

Notes

Recipe Name			
Serves	Prep Time	Cooking Time	Oven Temp

Ingredients

Directions

Notes

Recipe Name			
Serves	Prep Time	Cooking Time	Oven Temp

Ingredients

Directions

Notes

Recipe Name			
Serves	Prep Time	Cooking Time	Oven Temp

Ingredients

Directions

Notes

Recipe Name			
Serves	Prep Time	Cooking Time	Oven Temp

Ingredients

Directions

Notes

Recipe Name			
Serves	Prep Time	Cooking Time	Oven Temp

Ingredients

Directions

Notes

Recipe Name			
Serves	Prep Time	Cooking Time	Oven Temp

Ingredients

Directions

Notes

Recipe Name			
Serves	Prep Time	Cooking Time	Oven Temp

Ingredients

Directions

Notes

Recipe Name			
Serves	Prep Time	Cooking Time	Oven Temp

Ingredients

Directions

Notes

Recipe Name			
Serves	Prep Time	Cooking Time	Oven Temp

Ingredients

Directions

Notes

Recipe Name			
Serves	Prep Time	Cooking Time	Oven Temp

Ingredients

Directions

Notes

Recipe Name			
Serves	Prep Time	Cooking Time	Oven Temp

Ingredients

Directions

Notes

Recipe Name			
Serves	Prep Time	Cooking Time	Oven Temp

Ingredients

Directions

Notes

Recipe Name			
Serves	Prep Time	Cooking Time	Oven Temp

Ingredients

Directions

Notes

Recipe Name			
Serves	Prep Time	Cooking Time	Oven Temp

Ingredients

Directions

Notes

Recipe Name			
Serves	Prep Time	Cooking Time	Oven Temp

Ingredients

Directions

Notes

Recipe Name			
Serves	Prep Time	Cooking Time	Oven Temp

Ingredients

Directions

Notes

Recipe Name			
Serves	Prep Time	Cooking Time	Oven Temp

Ingredients

Directions

Notes

Recipe Name			
Serves	Prep Time	Cooking Time	Oven Temp

Ingredients

Directions

Notes

Recipe Name			
Serves	Prep Time	Cooking Time	Oven Temp

Ingredients

Directions

Notes

Recipe Name			
Serves	Prep Time	Cooking Time	Oven Temp

Ingredients

Directions

Notes

Recipe Name			
Serves	Prep Time	Cooking Time	Oven Temp

Ingredients

Directions

Notes

Recipe Name			
Serves	Prep Time	Cooking Time	Oven Temp

Ingredients

Directions

Notes

Recipe Name			
Serves	Prep Time	Cooking Time	Oven Temp

Ingredients

Directions

Notes

Recipe Name			
Serves	Prep Time	Cooking Time	Oven Temp

Ingredients

Directions

Notes

Recipe Name			
Serves	Prep Time	Cooking Time	Oven Temp

Ingredients

Directions

Notes

Recipe Name			
Serves	Prep Time	Cooking Time	Oven Temp

Ingredients

Directions

Notes

Recipe Name			
Serves	Prep Time	Cooking Time	Oven Temp

Ingredients

Directions

Notes

Recipe Name			
Serves	Prep Time	Cooking Time	Oven Temp

Ingredients

Directions

Notes

Recipe Name			
Serves	Prep Time	Cooking Time	Oven Temp

Ingredients

Directions

Notes

Recipe Name			
Serves	Prep Time	Cooking Time	Oven Temp

Ingredients

Directions

Notes

Recipe Name			
Serves	Prep Time	Cooking Time	Oven Temp

Ingredients

Directions

Notes

Recipe Name			
Serves	Prep Time	Cooking Time	Oven Temp

Ingredients

Directions

Notes

Recipe Name			
Serves	Prep Time	Cooking Time	Oven Temp

Ingredients

Directions

Notes

Recipe Name			
Serves	Prep Time	Cooking Time	Oven Temp

Ingredients

Directions

Notes

Recipe Name			
Serves	Prep Time	Cooking Time	Oven Temp

Ingredients

Directions

Notes

Recipe Name			
Serves	Prep Time	Cooking Time	Oven Temp

Ingredients

Directions

Notes

Recipe Name			
Serves	Prep Time	Cooking Time	Oven Temp

Ingredients

Directions

Notes

Recipe Name			
Serves	Prep Time	Cooking Time	Oven Temp

Ingredients

Directions

Notes

Recipe Name			
Serves	Prep Time	Cooking Time	Oven Temp

Ingredients

Directions

Notes

Recipe Name			
Serves	Prep Time	Cooking Time	Oven Temp

Ingredients

Directions

Notes

Recipe Name			
Serves	Prep Time	Cooking Time	Oven Temp

Ingredients

Directions

Notes

Recipe Name			
Serves	Prep Time	Cooking Time	Oven Temp

Ingredients

Directions

Notes

Recipe Name			
Serves	Prep Time	Cooking Time	Oven Temp

Ingredients

Directions

Notes

Recipe Name			
Serves	Prep Time	Cooking Time	Oven Temp

Ingredients

Directions

Notes

Recipe Name			
Serves	Prep Time	Cooking Time	Oven Temp

Ingredients

Directions

Notes

Recipe Name			
Serves	Prep Time	Cooking Time	Oven Temp

Ingredients

Directions

Notes

Recipe Name			
Serves	Prep Time	Cooking Time	Oven Temp

Ingredients

Directions

Notes

Recipe Name			
Serves	Prep Time	Cooking Time	Oven Temp

Ingredients

Directions

Notes

Recipe Name			
Serves	Prep Time	Cooking Time	Oven Temp

Ingredients

Directions

Notes

Recipe Name			
Serves	Prep Time	Cooking Time	Oven Temp

Ingredients

Directions

Notes

Recipe Name			
Serves	Prep Time	Cooking Time	Oven Temp

Ingredients

Directions

Notes

Recipe Name			
Serves	Prep Time	Cooking Time	Oven Temp

Ingredients

Directions

Notes

Photographs

Photographs / Notes

Photographs / Notes

Photographs / Notes

Photographs / Notes

Photographs / Notes

Need another Recipe Journal?

Visit www.blankbooksnjournals.com

47659242R00068

Made in the USA
Lexington, KY
11 December 2015